A Golden Friendship

Poems of Faith, Hope and Sunday Dinner

MELVIN W. DONAHO, PhD

authorHOUSE®

AuthorHouse™
1663 Liberty Drive
Bloomington, IN 47403
www.authorhouse.com
Phone: 1 (800) 839-8640

Published by AuthorHouse 06/05/2018

ISBN: 978-1-5462-4430-1 (sc)
ISBN: 978-1-5462-4428-8 (hc)
ISBN: 978-1-5462-4429-5 (e)

Library of Congress Control Number: 2018906439

Print information available on the last page.

Contents

Dear Readers,

Over the years I have been privileged to write this collection of poetry; at first for my adored bride, now called to her eternal rest, and as an outlet for my own feelings, memories and deep beliefs. The great majority of these poems emerged from a sense of sincerity. I also hope that each of you might be motivated to share your own feelings, memories and beliefs as a personal outlet and as moments of quiet enjoyment. The first poem, *A Golden Friendship* was written for my much loved bride of sixty years. A young reviewer wrote: "I only wish that I could have a relationship like this." I was surprised and honored that this poem, so dear to me, received a 4.5 rating by well over 150 reviewers. My primary desire is that each of you enjoy and reflect on each of these works which was so often the result of a deep love and sense of truth. My heartfelt love to each of you. Recalling that wonderful poem, *Kubla Khan,* by Samuel Taylor Coleridge, I, too, want only to be counted as one who loves his fellow man. When it comes to assistance, help and comments. I am truly grateful to Susan Quam who made a major contribution in typing and assisting in so many ways; and, to Audrey Williams and Karen Bennett for their support and insights in reading the final drafts.

Sincerely,
Mel Donaho

Dedicated To
My Beloved Wife

Ruth Gronert Donaho
October 4, 1933 – September 23, 2015

It is with deep appreciation that the author acknowledges Susan Quam for her typing and proofreading of this work.

A Golden Friendship

To: Ruth
On Our Golden Anniversary

A wise man once wrote these eternal words of truth:
"Marry someone whose soul you've come to love,
For passion fades ...
But friendship lasts forever."

After fifty golden years with you, dear Ruth,
These words are engraved deep within
My heart as truth.
Yes, golden friendship has long endured
And kept its luster throughout the years;
And this is why I treasure still your golden love.

Just over fifty years ago today, I asked
For your hand, to hear you say,
"You'll have to ask my Dad if it's O.K."
And, so I did. And after a merry chase
Along the path, I cornered him to hear him laugh,
"What did my daughter say?"
"Why, sir," I then replied, seeing the twinkle in his eye,
"that I must seek your permission."

"My son, you have my consent on this condition:
That you take good care of her,
Treat her tenderly with love
Know that her Mother and I are here for you as well."

We took our vows and prayed to God above.
Wealth and treasure had we none,
Nor even a house to call our home;
But, we were rich beyond compare with Golden love.
Our Golden love has long endured
And kept its luster through the years,
And, we've been rich beyond compare with Golden love.
Just as a rose so precious and so fair,
Is the golden friendship that we've shared.
It was planted with caring and warmed by the sun,
We've known infinite sharing, laughter and fun.

We've shared many blessings and it isn't hard to see;
That life's most valued pleasures
Were bountiful and free.
It isn't what we own nor treasure
That signifies a measure of our wealth …
But, those special gifts from God which know no price:
Our family, friends, and health.

We know not what tomorrow brings
Nor how long we have left.
Our faith is based not on believing that God can;
But in knowing that He will.
And, in days to come, that we'll be truly blessed,
With a love enriched by a golden friendship
Beyond our fondest dreams to share.

Dear Ruth, know that should you become sad;
I'll dry your tears.
Should you become frightened;
I'll comfort your fears.
Should you become worried;
You may turn to me for hope.
Or, should you become confused or lost,
I'll be there to help you cope.

You have my heart,
I'll hold your hand.
You'll know my love until the end.
Ah, yes, you have my love,
My all, my golden friend.

By: Mel Donaho

A Cultural Perspective

To: Waldo C Donaho

Ere long ago, a man was praised;
For his words, here paraphrased:
"Flower in a crannied wall,
I pluck you out, root and all.
If I could understand what you are,
I should know what God and man is."
His western thought is oft perceived
As a model logic for us to see.
Yet, in a far, far eastern land,
A humble man, though not so grand,
Knelt and gazed in silent awe,
At a flower near an ancient wall.
Then shared this immortal thought for all:
"Oh, lovely flower growing free,
I bow to thee on humble knee.
If I could grasp your loveliness,
'Twould bring eternal bliss and set me free."

Thus, from these opposite lands on Earth,
We see two views evolved from birth.
In each a flower plays center stage;
In each a thought is posed – quite sage.
At first, we're quick to criticize;
Impose our thoughts to which is wise.
Too often we think we know what's best;
Even though our thoughts have met no test.
When weighing in balance these philosophies,
Let's not judge – approve – condemn –
The writings of such mortal men.
But seek through wisdom to understand,
The differences in cultures of these lands.

By: Mel Donaho

Motivation for Writing *A Cultural Perspective*

As we grow older, our perspectives often change. For years I resented Tennyson's "Flower in a crannied Wall" and felt it inferior in thought when he "plucks out the flower roots and all." How much more admirable, I felt, was the unknown, eastern poet who only admired his flower growing free. Today, who am I to judge their heartfelt works through my modern eyes? Now, as I re-think their words, it becomes apparent that the cultural insights revealed within their thoughts are much more significant in seeking to understand their diverse cultures. Is not their view of each flower a means to revealing a higher, greater, though different end? With this in mind, I dedicate this poem to my brother, Waldo, who recently wrestled with his own doubts and fears of what lies hereafter. Now, he knows; but, us? We'll have to wait.

A Love Filled Heart

A love filled heart broke tonight
Recalling its mate; no more in sight.
There was no stopping tears that flowed;
From deep inside, they overflowed.
For the past two years she's been asleep;
Resting in her Savior's grace; no cause to weep.
Tomorrow marks the day that she was born;
A day for which I'll forever thank you, Lord;
For our sixty years of sweet accord;
For the lovely woman whom I adore.
I know I owe You for my very life;
As well as for my sainted wife's.
And now, Dear Savior I turn to Thee;
Praying that one day our Souls
Might rise from Bedford's depths;
To be with Thee for all Eternity.

By: Melvin Donaho
October 3, 2017

A Poem for Seth

Disney has his bouncing Tigger
Far outbounced by Seth, by jigger!
Flamboyant, gyroscoping boy;
Turning cartwheels – full of joy.

Oh, at times, he's quite a charmer;
Big wide smile – a five alarmer!
There are times he acts quite coy;
And, at others – he's all BOY.

Ask his sister, if you please;
And she'll tell you he's a tease.
He's a terror with a water gun;
But, there's no doubt, he's having fun.

To be fair, he's tall and lean;
A future athlete – it would seem.
He'll be a challenge to his teachers;
And, a full-time vigil for a preacher.

There is no question – he's a boy;
Who brings his family the greatest joy.
We'll root for him and patch his knees;
We'll love him while we search for keys!

By: Mel Donaho
April 17, 2003

A Requiem to Love

Dedicated to Audrey and to My Dear Love

For sixty years I loved your sister;
As you did love your Herm.
Then our Savior called him to eternal rest.
He had served his Lord; had met His tests.
I remember, oh so well, his gift of song;
With which he lovingly praised his Lord.
His caring wife oft sang in choir with him
And now dear Lord, I pray;
Please, take good care of him.
A few years later, my Ruth was also blessed;
Called by her Savior to her eternal rest.
Surely, like Herm, she'd served her Lord;
Had done her very best.
The day before Christ called her home;
She handed me Job's robe and said;
"It is finished, my Love;
Please, do not cancel this drama of our Lord;
Its message is too great;
And your ability to direct too strong."
I promised both my love and God;
That I would do my best.
One last time she turned to me and said:
"My Love, you've been wonderful;
Just wonderful to me."
And lo, she then passed into eternity.
Now, Dear Audrey, we must wait
'Til God calls us through Heaven's Gate.
Now, I do pray that just inside
Our Lord and loved ones do await.

By: Melvin Donaho

As if it Were Just Yesterday

Just yesterday we met, my love;
Brought together by God above.
How I remember that sudden storm
As if it were just yesterday!
Seeking the comfort of a nearby inn;
Our lives together did just begin –
As if it were just yesterday.
Unaware 'twas God's plan for us;
We built a lasting, mutual trust.
We were not blessed with any wealth;
Just our God, our friends, our health.
I found the library, a special treat;
For it was there we'd often meet.
It was first there, I do recall,
I kissed my maid from Lincoln Hall.
As if it were just yesterday.
And when I asked her to be my wife;
To join with me; to share my life.
I was surprised to hear her say;
You'll have to ask my Dad, if it's okay.
Indeed, I would; but first I'd pray.
I remember as if it were just yesterday.
After leading me a merry chase,
I finally caught him face to face;
And with a twinkle in his eye, he did reply:
"What did my daughter say?"
Why sir, that I must first seek your okay.

"Her Mother and I welcome you, our son;
For we know our daughter's love you've won."
I remember, as if it were just yesterday.
And then an angel without wings,
Floated down an aisle to join with me.
'Twas then I knew true ecstasy.
Our Lord was very good to us;
He placed two children in our trust.
And we became a family.
I remember as if it were just yesterday.
We progressed through our life together;
Meeting no challenge, we could not weather.
Three score years quickly sped by;
Then came that fateful day in May.
When we did hear the doctor say:
My dear, your cancer is stage four
For which there is no cure in store.
I remember as if it were just yesterday.
I prayed and prayed it was not true;
However, God was calling you.
The night before you passed away,
You smiled at me, an angelic way.
With love shining in your eyes –
A smile upon your lips; you said to me:
"My love, you've been wonderful;
Just wonderful for me."
Her final words to me – you see.
The following day, my love went home;
Called forever by Christ alone.
I remember as if it were just yesterday.
And now I await my Lord above;
To join us once again in love;
As if it were just yesterday.

By: Mel Donaho

14

"By day the Lord directs his love,
At night his song is with me –
A prayer to the God of my life."
Psalm 42:8

Each morning sorrow greets me
As I awake and start my day.
But, I know God's love will sooth me
and bless me as I pray.

The following stanza is the refrain after each stanza.
Yes, I know His loving kindness,
Will brush away my tears.
I remember my Savior's promise
Which helps to ease my fears.

When I feel quite discouraged,
I look up and pray to Him.
I think of my Savior's love,
And am thankful deep within.

Prayers and memories fill my day.
As I lay down alone.
I sing praises to my Lord;
For the love He'd sent my way.

By: Melvin Donaho

Note: This poem was set to music and performed during the 8:00am service of Life in Christ Lutheran Church. The poem was set to music by Pat Herman, LICL organist and was sung by Connie Baker, frequent LICL soloist. Their duet was beautiful and moved the author to tears. The 2nd paragraph was rewritten as the refrain for each of the other stanzas.

By: Melvin Donaho

Camp Bedford Respite

There is a magnetism that draws one to thy shores.
Memories of past moments spent tingle every pore.
Where on this day could an hour more happily be spent
Then viewing thy beauty beneath the cloak of winter's bent?
Only the track of one lone skier transcends thy hidden ponds.
Ponds which soon will reflect countless youthful faces,
Storing memories for future eternities;
Ponds whose shores share memories of contented love
Gazing hand in hand
While drinking of thy magic wonders and of each other.
Ah, yes, my memory, drink thy fill and dream of times to come –
Not yet in bloom.
Dream of spring's flowers waiting to burst forth,
Of loving smiles to be shared and re-shared
Through reflections of deep, mutual love.
Bedford, there are no shamrocks upon they shores,
But leprechauns do there abound,
And even within depths of dancing eyes are found.
While one knows not what the future has in store,
I would my ashes one day sift to thy pond's floor.

By: Mel Donaho

God Called You Home

A few years ago today, God called you home.
While I was left behind; but not alone.
Our Lord still watches over me
Blessed with two children – memories of thee.
One day my faith will also set me free.
And, God willing, I'll be joined again with thee.
Until then, I shall rejoice in Life in Christ;
Thankful for our many Christian friends.
With whom to pray, to worship Christ our Lord.
One year ago today, our Pastor sat with you and me
And prayed;
And prayed;
And prayed.
His words, his prayers helped send your soul,
To be entered on our Lord's eternal roll.
Here today, my Love, I pray for you,
Knowing that you are at rest;
That in Christ's arms you've met the test.

By: Melvin Donaho

My heartfelt thanks to Pastor George Spicer, a true servant of our Lord, and to all the members of Life of Christ who have comforted and supported me throughout the years. It was Ruth who sewed all the costumes for our dramas to include Job's robe the afternoon before she was called to rest. And, it was she who gave me the idea for developing *An Evening with Martin Luther.*

God Hears Believers' Prayers

A few days later at home in the Florida Keys;
Terry McGhee went down on one knee;
While holding her hand in a light gentle squeeze;
He looked deep into her eyes and said;
Mary, will you marry me, please;
And be my bride in these Florida Keys?
Oh, Terry, I already said I'd be your
Loving wife for the rest of my life.
Yes, my Dear Mary; but now your finger will carry
A token of my sincerest love for you.
With tears in her eyes she gave a deep sigh;
Embraced in his arms; she was quick to reply;
Oh Terry, how much I love you.
Well, Terry said to his Mary;
Let's share with my brother our very good news
Timothy's the sadist of clowns in the big center ring.
Here he comes now; but he's looking like doom
Oh, Terry, I feel like it too;
The girl that I loved; I've now come to rue.
She's run off with the banker you see.
And she's left me behind with a note and her ring.
To her, money talked loudly and Paris a fling.
Oh Timothy, I'm sorry; but I'm sure you can see;
That she wasn't the girl; God meant you to meet.

So, Terry hugged his brother and left him to grieve;
To talk about how they might help his brother, Timothy.
They no more than sat down when Mary with a smile;
Said, Terry, I know just the girl for your brother Timothy.
Terry brightened and asked her what did she mean?
Why my sister, Julie, who's younger than me.
She is lovely, witty, and bright as can be.
I think our Lord would approve; if we prayed it to be.
So Mary and Terry bowed their heads to their Lord;
And prayed that He'd bless the ones they loved best.
Then Mary and Terry came up with their plan;
That they would meet separately at Ol' Trader Dan's.
They prayed again their Lord's support of their devious plan.
That Julie and Timothy might find each other just grand.
While they viewed each other with eyes of delight;
Terry excused himself to meet with a friend;
And, Mary excused herself to go with Terry.
Later that evening, the four met once again.
Only this time Julie and Timothy wore the biggest of grins.
And Julie gave Mary the biggest of hugs and proclaimed;
My Dear conniving sister we will keep our same names;
But now we have a question to ask of you two;
Do you think a double wedding might do?

By: Melvin Donaho

God Hears Our Prayers

There was a young man on a flying trapeze
He flew through the air like a soft gentle breeze.
He went to God's house; where he prayed on his knees;
Did this daring young man from the flying trapeze.
He prayed to his Lord that he might be blessed;
With a lovely young lass who could love him the best
It was an all loving God who did hear his request.
And lo! Down the aisle, she floated, well blessed;
Then entered his pew; all dressed in white lace.
She looked; then she smiled with a shy grin on her face.
At that moment he fell; his heart she did win.
The Pastor ended his sermon and prayers;
He ended his message, by stating, "God really cares."
And the newly met couple left with less cares.
When, out near the street – before he could speak
With tears in her eyes, she gave a deep sigh;
And said, you're my kind of guy; but you see I cannot lie;
There's no future for us; tomorrow I leave for the Florida Keys.
Elated he cried; with bright sparkling eyes;
May our Savior be blessed, he heard my request.
Once again she replied with tears in her eyes;
I don't understand why you're so happy and pleased;
When we'll be so far apart with me in the Florida Keys.
No, I'll be there with you; then you will know it is true;
I'm the young lad, above, on the flying trapeze.

Now, I know who you are. For I've watched from afar;
With you astride, I watched your proud horses arrive.
In the future I see, you'll be riding with me.
You see, I've truly been blessed; by our Savior's largess.
But now she replied, with her tears now all dry;
Assuming we marry, what name will I carry?
Oh yes, you might wonder; I'm Mary McCarry;
Who, out of the blue, has fallen for you.
Oh, Mary McCarry, I'm Terry McGee, and yes it is true,
Our Lord brought the two of us together.
And when we do marry; we'll praise our Savior anew.
All the while God watched from Heaven above;
For He knew what their future would be.

By: Melvin Donaho

Happiness – The Test of Man

If man could live content within his means –
Seeking simplicity rather than luxury; or, so it seems;
He could know happiness.
If man could seek refinement rather than fashion;
Worthiness rather than self-serving – quite ashen;
He could know happiness.
For what is happiness in inner man,
If it is not the freedom to think;
To hear all with an open mind or heart?
And, surely, to seek the greater good;
To encourage the spiritual to grow –
To find its way to diffuse an inner peace?
Is it not to give unselfishly; each in his own measure
Of knowledge, love, and charity?
To know that one did his best –
Even though thousands still stand in need;
Even though hatred and bigotry still co-exist;
Even though, yes, even though the patient died;
And, yet, one did his best?
Surely, true happiness is the test of man.

By: Mel Donaho
July 2000

I Come to You, Oh Lord

Dedicated to
Eileen and Anthony Bieneman

I come to you, Oh Lord;
I come to you in prayer.
I come to you, Oh Lord;
Because I know you're there.
Because I know your love and care;
Dear Lord, I offer you my days;
Cast off my sins and evil ways.
I offer you my pleasures and my joys;
Lord, I also offer up my sorrow;
My pains, my fears and all tomorrows.
This evening I bow my head to Thee;
Praying Dear Savior, you'll set me free
When you called my love to be with Thee;
I prayed Dear Lord; that you'd call me;
I realize that that could never be;
For you have your plans designed for me.
Lord, while I'm here upon this Earth;
I'll teach your Word for all I'm worth.
When you've finally to me called;
May I be worthy; may I not fall.
Amen

By: Melvin Donaho
August 15, 2017

I Know Not the Road

I know not the road you took, my love;
I only know it carried you to Heaven above.
It is the one I pray, that one day I, too, will take.
Then, hand in hand before our Lord we'll stand.
Humbly pleading forgiveness for our sins;
Knowing His Son died for our salvation;
And for those of every nation.

By: Melvin Donaho

I'm Your Dad: Yes, I'm Your Friend

Ah, my Dear, I'm confident
Two hearts can make amends;
So you may always know –
I'm your Dad; and, yes, your friend.

The differences in generation
We can both transcend.
Let's always talk and walk together –
I'm your Dad; and, yes, your friend.

Although it's time to test your wings
And, be a sampler of many things;
Remember, I am always there –
I'm your Dad; and, yes, your friend.

And as you ponder each new choice
May you have cause to pause, rejoice;
Knowing you can always turn to –
Your ol' Dad, and yes, your friend.

There is a sense of love and warmth
On which we both depend.
Thus, I may say with heartfelt fondness –
I'm your Dad; and, yes, your friend.

The bond which we will build with time
Is one which knows no end.
In fact, it grows much stronger –
I'm your Dad; and, yes, your friend.

By: Melvin Donaho

In Full Dress

Black clouds billow and fill the sky;
The loud winds howl and leaves fly by.
Lightning flashes in spears of fire;
Torrential rains turn dust to mire.

The thirsty desert deep its fill;
While swollen streams rush through its hills.
Desert plants change from brown to green;
The great Saguaro cacti seem to preen.

The rains pour down for two days or more;
Soaking, replenishing the desert floor.
Gradually, the morning light shines through;
Wondrously, the sky turns blue.

The rising sun reflects from hills of fire;
Bold colors vibrate – wild flowers inspire.
Travelers, in wonder, stop to rest;
To view God's desert – in full dress.

By: Mel Donaho
September 2000

Introspection

As I think of thoughts to share, my son,
I'm reminded of how my life has run.
In all I've pursued, there's been one voice –
To do my best, to make the right choice,
To believe in a philosophy that my fellow man
Must be taught and guided in a sound life plan.
Our duty to man we cannot duck,
Yet we owe so much to old Lady Luck.
Pick the minds of the thinkers and learn from the best;
Stand firm in the pursuit of your life-long quest!
Remember, consult with those you'd lead;
Learn to be tolerant – understand their needs.
Be considerate – delegate to them the task;
Ere they reflect faces of apathy – at best a mask.
Where current success if firmly found,
You may either stay afloat or go aground.
My son, look not to the status quo to seek your fame,
Recognize, resolve obstacles, and build your name.
Apologize to no man when you've tried your best,
Give credit to all men when you've passed the test.

By: Mel Donaho

Legacy

To: Jennifer and Seth

Life seems much more difficult today;
Than when we passed along this way.
There was so much for us to do;
Mow lawns – even milk a cow or two.
Outings with family to the lake;
The joy of catching a fish to bake.
Dreaming of having children; well, just a few.
With no thought of a life we'd come to rue.
With two lovely grandchildren we've been blessed.

Yet, life seems much more difficult today;
Than when we passed along this way.
Computers and television with their glitter,
Have pursued and won – their babysitter!
It's a challenge and quite true;
To encourage them to go to school.
Now, I share with the two I love best
These words before I go to rest.

Life seems more difficult today;
Than when we passed along this way.
To you dear Jenny and dear Seth,
I challenge you to do your best.
Study hard; learn to read and write.
Learn to speak with power, poise, and might.

Others around you may do quite well;
But, those with skill to speak and write excel!
Look for challenges along the way;
Those well-worn paths will make you pay!
Remember, to your Lord to pray.
Never doubt Him; come what may.

Life seems more difficult today;
Than when we passed along this way.
Two more thoughts I'd share with you;
First, strive to do your best in all you do.
Dare to fail but bounce back true;
Higher and higher until you reach the crest;
And, know that you've achieved your best!

Second, life was not meant to be lived alone;
But choose a mate to build a home.
Choose wisely; yes, choose a friend;
Who'll stand beside you to the end.
Say NO to that which would hold you back;
Embrace all that keeps you on the right track.
Know that your life will be more difficult in time;
Than when I wrote for you this rhyme.

By: Mel Donaho

Lord, I Am Ready

Dear Lord, I am ready, please, call me home
On bended knees I'll greet You; I'll gladly come.
Lord, You've freely given me the greatest joys in life;
Your loving Son, crucified, and my loving wife.
Since that day You called her Home;
I've prayed and prayed and prayed.
I'm sure You've heard my prayers, Oh, Lord.
I'm sure I've heard You say;
"Be patient, my son; it won't be long,
Your turn will come, just pray."
I turned to her picture on the wall;
She smiled and seemed to say;
"My Dear, look to our Triune God.
Listen to what He'll say. As we held hands;
Drank His blood and ate His bread, we prayed:
Dearest Lord, we've read Your Word;
We believe in Your Dear Son;
And pray for Your Grace today as one."
With such a gift from our Dear Lord;
Know now just why I pray;
I love my Lord, believe His Word;
Long before those days.
And now I look to Heaven above,
To be with her again, hand in hand, as one
Praising our Lord again.

By: Melvin Donaho

Mast Timber

A Tribute to Pastor Spicer

Our Lord made mountains with tall peaks,
And silent sentinels on their sides.
Strong mast timber for great ships;
Such, is the tall white pine.
Mast timber is also found in man;
As in our Pastor, in our life span.
Our tall leader, here today;
Who patiently leads us as we pray.
Neither pine nor man are quickly made;
Both are formed and tempered,
By God and the tests of time;
Years of our Lord's most careful tuning.
Brings forth that magic touch of greatness;
Lifting lofty tree and man,
Far above the heights of lesser masses;
Tall leaders destined to billow forth.
Inspiring the paths of thousands.
Great ships you have your lofty pines;
With wisdom, friend and grace
In God and our Pastor find.

By: Mel Donaho

Moments to Cherish

Yesterday – a pony-tailed lass
With sunshine on her face,
Filled with laughter – agile, flowing grace.
Yesterday – a flashing lass,
Whizzing by on skis,
Filled with vigor – band-aids on her knees.
Yesterday – a lovely bride,
Dressed in regal white,
Filled with joy – her chosen at her side.
Today – our daughter and our son,
Facing life together,
Filled with hope – while seeking boundless treasure.
And now – a bubbling little girl
Filled with smiles and glee,
A pony-tailed lass, perched on Grandpa's knee!

By: Melvin Donaho

My Dearest Friends

After fifty years of wedded bliss,
You look so happy to have faced life's risks.
Please, tell us what did you do?
To face life's challenges –
To remain so true?
Before even we were wed;
We discussed what should we do;
To make our marriage last.
First, we had our faith in God;
Without it we would rue.
Then, there were a few things;
Needed to keep our marriage true.
We both agreed our Mothers, dear;
Could be an awful pain.
Each wanted us to be quite near;
With them on holidays.
We knew that that would never do;
We came up with a plan or two,
Our first holiday would be her Mom's
And alternate the rest.
We invited them into our nest;
And shared with each our very best.
But, what else did you do?

We agreed that compliments,
Would help us achieve our best.
I was an excellent cook; my love did learn
I encouraged her she'd do just fine.
However, she could not seem to grasp
Why I liked most burnt toast.
With a hug and sweet caress;
I assured her what I loved best.
You should know that it did not matter;
A new blouse, a skirt, and, yes, burnt toast;
I complimented her. Toast, you say?
That became a hearty laugh one day.
We did things together.
And she had her activities and I had mine.
Decisions we did share,
With loving tender care.
We never went to bed with questions unresolved.
Our success? We loved each other dearly.

By: Melvin Donaho

My Final Bow

Dear Friends-my family-here at Life in Christ;
It is with tears I write to you.
Our Lord dictates our fates as He has mine.
It was our Lord who chose this home
For Ruth and me.
Our Lord, who chose you; our family.
It was our pleasure and gift to share with you
Our talents – to lead our fellow members to excel
In sharing *The Lord's Last Supper;*
And *The Book of Job.*
As you know, God called Ruth home;
And left me behind but not alone.
Today, I humbly take my final bow.
To depart my love, to move to my
Daughter's in Las Vegas.
Now that I have said my final lines;
Performance just a memory –
For reasons kept silently, deep within,
I will also have taken my final bow with Him.
I've owed my Savior all my life;
To do my best in spite of strife.
God willing, I shall be blessed;
To teach His Words 'til called to rest.
Goodbye my Christian friends but
I shall try to visit when I can. May
God continue to bless our wonderful
Pastors who meant so much to me.
May God bless you one and all.

By: Melvin Donaho

Ogden Nash – Revisited

"Candy is dandy;
But, liquor is quicker",
Ol' Oggie once wrote.
Reflects the thinking
Of a feckless, young goat!
The best persuasion,
If, I'm not remiss,
Begins with a simple,
Soft, stolen kiss.
If in a hurry,
Oggie's way may well do.
But for the long haul,
His way may one rue!
(Perhaps, with more than
A black eye or two!)
Ah yes, begin with a kiss;
Perhaps, one more than a few;
Then, one may find a mate,
For a lifetime to woo.

By: Mel Donaho

Oh, What Have I Heard

Oh, what have I heard listening to my soul …
The quiet sounds
Of fingers brushing on my cheek.
The loud sounds
Of the pounding of a love-filled heart.
The gentle sounds
Of whispered love from deep within.
The soft, wet sounds
Of falling, heartfelt tears.

Oh, what have I found through knowledge of my soul …
The true meaning of sharing life together.
The building of
A deep, abiding trust.
The very essence of
Our bonded bliss.
The knowledge of
A forever happiness.

Oh, what have I seen seeing through my soul …
The loveliness of your gentle face.
The vibrant pulsing of your beating heart.
The very soul of you through deepest eyes.
The true meaning of love reflected back to me.
Ah! Yes, my soul …
I have listened.
I have learned.
I have seen …
And I thank God for you
My dearest love.

By: Melvin Donaho

Once Again, My Love

Two years have passed us by
Since the day your soul from thee did fly.
I watched you take your final breath;
As God called your soul to be at rest.
I bowed my head and cried;
And cried;
And cried.
With tears flowing from my eyes,
Quietly, friends led me from your side;
No longer would I view you; now well blessed;
Yet, knowing that with Christ, you'd met His test;
Then our children, family and our friends;
Did join with me;
As our beloved Pastor blessed your ashes;
Which now reside in care with me.
Awaiting our mutual final destiny;
To rest together beneath Camp Bedford Pond;
Beside whose shores we served
Our youth, our friends, our Lord.
Oh, Bedford, you masterpiece of God!
One day again, my Love and I shall rely on thee:
Hold us in your depths;
Until our Lord and Savior calls us;
To be with Him, together, in Eternity.
Amen

By: Melvin Donaho

Our Daughter

Dedicated to Kathy

Dark hair flying,
Eyes ablazing,
Foot-feed to the floor;
Philosopher of Whitman's chocolates,
Sampling each – and often more.

Tell her not in mournful numbers
Of Oedipus and Merrick!
Point her to the halls of ovens,
There to bake her cake and share it!

Liberal education is not icing on her cake;
To her it's just one big headache!
Ah yes! French is for the Frenchies;
Math is just one big mistake!

Lead her to the halls of braising;
There her efforts are amazing.
There she shows a reckless glee –
(Even though she'll burn her knee!)

Breads, pies and cakes are her forte.
Accounting, English are her morte!
Flour, spices and sugar are her tools;
While numbers, verbs are fit for fools!

Dark hair flying,
Eyes ablazing,
Foot feed to the floor.
Philosopher of Whitman's chocolates.
Sampling each – and often more!

By: Mel Donaho

Our Own Bouquet

Dedicated to Herm and Audrey

Much needed rain soaks the desert floor;
Bringing forth flowers by the thousands or more.
This desert bouquet thanks God above;
For showering down His abundant love.

A scared, feeble dog seeks to creep away;
An old man calls, "Come, boy. It's OK."
He offers it some milk in a pail;
And, is justly rewarded by the wag of its tail.

A spouse for more than several years;
Calms her mate of his deepest fears.
A life-threatening illness has just been found;
They each share a love that knows no bounds.

Let us remember as we pass each day;
To treat each with kindness along our way.
The kindnesses returned will soon repay –
We'll have thousands of flowers – our own bouquet.

By: Mel Donaho

Requiem

Now, as I near my last days
To my Savior, I'll pray;
Please, forgive me my sins
For which on the cross, You did say;
"Father, forgive them their sins;
They know not what they do."
And dear Lord, I know it is true;
And now:
I have written my poems.
I've played my final act as;
The Bard would have me to do.
And I write this prose, for
It is my legacy to you.
And now …
I write my life's story,
As the curtain slowly falls
And I pray for God's forgiveness
At my final curtain call.

By: Melvin Donaho

Round and Round They Weave

Planets speed across the sky;
Yet, always pass the others by.
Round and round and round they weave,
Rarely causing need to grieve.
Here on Earth such is not so;
The unknown is met where'er we go.
Bodies clash both night and day;
Fusing – unwilling to pass or go their way.
Man meets woman and in a glance,
Love radiates – while hearts entrance.
Complications do then arise;
Each should have passed the other by.
Round and round and round they weave;
Deeply caring need meets need.
So much is due to circumstance;
So much must be decreed to chance.
While planets speed across the sky,
Yet, always pass the others by.
Humanoids more wobbly go,
Creating havoc, heartache, woe.

By: Mel Donaho

One never knows where the inspiration for a poem might arise. "Round and Round they Weave" was motivated when I substituted for an eleventh grade English teacher for three weeks. She had assigned her students to write a personal type essay which I had the pleasure of grading. At least one half of the students wrote about sexual based problems in their homes or lives. From this experience, the inspiration for this poem emerged.

Savior, Help Me to Pray

Savior, I bow my head to You in prayer;
But, I am often lost and meet a snare.
I know the prayer your Son did teach.
Yet, beyond it seems so out of reach.
Oh, Father I would talk with thee;
Share all my concerns for you to see.
Dear Lord, I do not want to know
What plans you have for me in store.
But I do implore your help to live,
Closer to You; much more to give.
Lord, since living upon this Earth;
I've been blessed fully since my birth.
To You, I must confess with shame;
The sins I've committed – some in Your name.
You've been so generous to me,
Yet, I've been blind and could not see;
Your gift of Christ upon that tree
And now I know, I'm sinless, free.
Still, Lord, it's so difficult for me;
To bow my head on bended knee,
To confess my sins, give praise to Thee.
Lord, I shall try again this day;
To share my thoughts with You.
Forgive my stumbles as I say;
What's in my heart, in my own way.

By: Melvin Donaho

Superstition or Dream?

It
Is readily
Apparent that the
Number thirteen inflames man –
Some to heights of superstition;
Others to deeper, more private dreams.
Do not confuse superstition with private dreams.
Superstition is for the mindless; dreams dare reality.
Is it not possible to view, say, December 13th
As being an omen of long sought for positive relations;
As opposed to a day to be dismally avoided and feared?
Of all the days of the year, December 13th should be special –
It should, as all thirteens, be shared with the warmth of a friend.
Should you be superstitious or afraid,
Come dream with me the dreams of reality!

Postscript:
If you think of that other "evil" number, eight, as in "dirty 8," or "behind the
eight ball," and add it to 13 – what do you get? December 21st! The luckiest
of days.

Happy birthday, Sweetheart!
Dad

By: Mel Donaho
December 13, 1987

Teach Our Children

Let's write a poem about Christmas!
For our children so bright and gay.
To remind them, Christ our Savior
Was born on Christmas day.
To Him be all honor and glory;
To Him let us bow and pray.
With Him let's share what's in our hearts;
As we celebrate Christmas day.
We ask, Lord, protect our children,
From the temptations on which them prey.
Help us teach them the true meanings of Christmas;
Often lost and forgotten today.
Teach them the tree we love to adorn;
Reflects our everlasting hope – not scorn.
Teach them the star which shines on high;
Is the sign of our Savior's birth.
Teach them that star shining bright in the sky;
Guided shepherds and wise men
To the place of His lowly birth.
Teach them the candles shining so brightly;
Reflect Christ, the light of the world.
Let them know full measure,
His warmth and love unfurled.
Be sure, when you hang the wreath upon your door;
To teach them love for one another, no matter how rich or poor.
Tell them – teach God's children the true
Meaning of Christmas night.
Teach them that the glitter and temptations
Which surround them;
Pale when weighed against Christ's holy light.

By: Melvin Donaho

The Final Bow

Quite soon I shall take my final bow;
While it lasted, it was oh so sweet.
Words of Luther will linger in my heart;
Far removed from "Papa is All, my first start.

I shall say my final words on stage,
For my church and for our Lord –
Both much adored, I shall remember
Earlier days and days that went before.

When I have said my final lines;
Performance just a memory –
For reasons kept silently, deep within,
I will have taken my final bow with him.

I've owed my Savior all my life;
To do my best in spite of strife.
God willing, I shall be blessed;
To teach His Words "til called to rest."

By: Melvin Donaho

The Honey Quest

A big, brown bear is a magnificent beast;
A tree filled with honey is his special feast,
And when he's sleeping deep in his lair;
His dreams are filled with thoughts so fair.
Having tasted his honey and savored her flavor;
He knows what he wants; his thoughts never waver.
His memory awakes; he remembers a store;
Of goodness and sweetness he's tasted before.
He knows there's much bliss as he goes on his way;
For he lives, dreams and loves for the joys of each day.
While it's not widely known, bears are really quite smart;
They carry visions of honey deep in their heart.
At last he reaches his pot full of gold;
But, somehow, now he's shy and not bold.
Nowhere is there found such honey as this;
To fill ol' bear with such rapture and bliss.
His honey demurs; but waits to be kissed;
And, ol' bear responds and learns what he's missed.
Yes sir, there's honey and there's honey;
But, no honey like this!

By: Mel Donaho

The Power of Faith

Not too many years ago; our Lord looked down
And saw a small devoted little flock;
United in a common bond and goal;
Determined to convert a former home
Into a place of worship for Him alone.
Surely, the Lord with His amazing grace,
Blessed this flock and its Holy place.
They prayed to place their needed call;
The Lord did hear their humble prayers;
And from his chosen saints on earth –
He sent to them His very best.
Whose faith shown like a glowing star;
He now serves this flock both near and far.
For him – no sacrifice too great.
He soothes their sorrows, pain and fate.
The little flock grew and grew,
Immersed in God's Scriptures, faith and grace,
They recognized their need for much more space.
Knowing that God would lead the way,
They built a Sanctuary so more might pray.
However, the status quo was not to be!
By them again a need was seen,
To create more space to teach and play.

This, too, became a cause to pray.
Led by a once small flock now grown,
With the power of faith in God alone.
Again God blessed this growing flock;
Whose dreams and visions no one mocked.
Life in Christ voted to serve their Lord.
To see their needs met in swift accord.
And, thus it is we see today,
This wondrous place to learn and play.
All praise and thanks be to you our Lord;
Through faith in Jesus rests our reward.

By: Melvin Donaho

The Saga of "Bear"

Squirrel chattered high in the tree;
"Bear, you're grouch as can be!"
Ol' Owl added with disdainful hoot;
"Bear, if I were bigger, I'd give you a boot!"

Black Crow flitted at an angry pace;
"Bear, why are you so down in the face?
Last month your singin' made a loud hullabaloo;
But, your singin' was better 'n this how-do-ya-do!"

Ol' Bear looked up and gave a sly sort of grin;
Like a little cub caught in his ol' Dad's gin.
"Now look here friends, I'm sure you'll understand –
I miss my Honey – straight grade "A" brand."

Squirrel scolded in a quite a loud voice;
"I know several honey trees, you can have your choice!"
"And, I know of five or six to boot,"
Ol' Owl added in a high-pitched hoot.

"There!" added Crow as he preened his black shroud.
"There wasn't any need to growl so loud!"
"Now, just a minute!" Bear shot right back.
"I know you mean well; but, you're on the wrong track!"

"I've found a *special* Honey tree –
Far better than that of any honey bee!
I know you mean quite well for me;
But, there's just no other "Honey" – can't you see?"

"Squirrel, you know just how it is;
I've watched you scamper after your own sweet Liz."
"And, you, Crow, you know full well,
That of all the Miss Crows, there's just one Belle."

"Remember how Owl acted like he'd been in the hooch?
And, hooted all day after just one smooch?"
"Now, in all fairness, I ask you three;
Don't I deserve my own special Honey tree?"

Ol' Owl found it difficult to swallow;
As he thought of his little "Hooter" in the hollow.
"OK! OK! Bear, we'll make you a deal;
Now that we understand just how you feel."

"You've kept us awake – can't get no sleep;
And our heads all ache 'til we want to weep.
We'll show you a place just over the bridge;
A lovely cave in a secluded ol' ridge."

"It's a great place you can call your own;
And, with a little effort it can be your home.
Bear, you can put your Honey's picture on the wall;
And, you can write your poems, sing, or have a ball!"

Ol' Bear smiled and was filled with glee;
His thoughts were inspired by what he could see.
He thought of all good times he could share;
While touching and smelling his Honey's hair.

Just what he's needed all these years!
A place and a friend to allay his fears.
Someone to share those quiet whiles;
Someone to exchange warm mutual smiles.

Ol' Bear started to dance a jig;
But, stubbed his toe on a great big twig;
As lay here, he thought quite long –
I know what I'll do! I'll write her a song!

As he lay there right on the ground;
The words began to come around!
He raised his voice unto the sky;
(One thing for sure, he wasn't shy!)

"Oh what a lovely morsel;
Oh what a memorable day!
My visions all are of my Honey;
Every moment along-ong the way."

"Oh what a tasty morsel;
Oh my what a loverly day!
Yes! My visions are all of Honey;
Every moment along the way-ay-ay!"

The Bluejays squawked – the squirrels barked;
Ol' Bear just waved, like he owned the park!
He was filled with Honey and he was filled with song;
All was right with *his* world, as he sang along.

He sang through the evening; and he sang all night.
He caused all the animals an awful fright!
Ol' Hoot Owl hooted that it still wasn't right;
To keep folks awake both day and night!

Maw Racoon felt great disdain;
And, called Ol' Bear a royal pain.
Jack Rabbit came out of his lair;
To tell Ol' Bear he wasn't quite fair.

Did Ol' Bear care? No siree. No siree!
He sang more boldly – but, still off key.
Then he began to improvise a bit;
Determined to write a woodland hit.

"She's a lovely honey tree, yum, yum, yum!
She's a lovely honey tree, yum, yum, yum!
She's a lovely honey tree;
She's a lovely honey tree ..."

Bear's singing quickly came to a rest –
As he gazed in wonder at the one he loved best.
His Honey tried hard not to laugh or smile;
But, it was tough; and, took her awhile.

"Bear, I'll happily go home with you –
But, your singing career must be through!
We need all our friends in this wooded bliss.
Then, with a warm heart, she sought his kiss.

By: Mel Donaho

The Saga of Goose

Written for Seth and Jenny

Someone forgot to close the gate!
Someone now was facing fate.
With its beak wide open; its neck extended –
Someone knew what was intended!
Ol' Goose charged with wings a flapping;
Someone tried fast backup backing!
Someone failed! Goose prevailed!
Battered, beaten, black and blue,
Someone ran away with rue.
Goose flapped his wings; called out in song;
Waddled in victory all day long!
Someone raced out; late for his game;
Goose charged again; not quite the same ...
Someone swung a bat with youthful zeal;
And, lo! Ol' Goose? Our Sunday meal.

By: Grandpa Donaho

Grandpa was motivated to write this poem based on a month on his Uncle Roy's farm. Ol' Goose was one nasty bird who didn't hesitate to attack anyone or anything to include Aunt Mary, the dogs, the cats, and Grandpa who was only nine years old back then. On the first "attack", Goose landed in the middle of Grandpa's back; biting, gouging and twisting his beak (which not only hurt but broke the skin and turned black and blue) and beating him with the hard bones in his wings. Believe me, the tears flew and all Grandpa could say was "Damned ol' Goose! I'll get even!" After the second, failed attack, Uncle Roy laughed, cleaned the Goose, and prepared it for Sunday dinner.

The Watermelon Man

Oh what music on a summer afternoon!
To hear the bells calling, "Watermelon Man!"
To hear the clippity clop of his horse drawing near;
To see Watermelon Man sitting cheerfully above his melons.
A sight of which paintings are all about;
Picturesque horse, with her ears sticking out
Like twin peaks through holes in an old Tyrolean hat.
Watermelon Man – what a joy!
Sitting there with his big watermelon smile,
Unbuttoned, faded plaid shirt and beat up old hat.
A boy's true friend; Boys who took deep pride
In calling, "Hey! Watermelon Man!"
"Mr. Watermelon Man, would you sell me a watermelon?"
"I've only got a dime."
"Whoa, Nellie." "Why son, a dime will buy you a real beauty!"
"But, didn't I see you across town last week?"
"Yes, Sir, I live 'bout two miles from here."
"Hmm, how are you gonna get that melon home?"
"It's for my Grandma and I'll take it to her;
She's been awful good to me; and, I'm strong."
Well, the boy hugged that melon to his chest;
And, began what would prove to be a test.
The first block he stepped out bold;
That big ol' melon in his hold.

About the third block he lost his swagger;
He stumbled and began to stagger.
With sweat flowing freely from his brow;
He managed two more blocks – somehow.
Tired and weary, he was forced to rest;
But, there was no quit; he'd try his best.
The sun was rising in the sky;
His dinner time was passing by.
Then he heard that sound he knew so well;
The clanging of Old Nellie's bell!
With a chuckle, Watermelon Man called out,
"Hey! Boy! Put your melon in the back;
Then scoot up here on this old sack."
Old Nellie pulled out at a steady gait;
Soon they were standing at his Grandma's gate.
Nellie's bell echoed down the street;
And, all the neighbors came out for treats!
When each and every melon had disappeared;
They hugged warmly as true friends should.
As the duo began their homeward way;
The boy sang out, his merriest;
"Hey! Watermelon Man, you're the greatest!"

By: Mel Donaho

The Wooden Bowl Revisited

Disturbed by their old Dad's carelessness;
Spilling, upsetting his food; making a mess.
Love filled their hearts as one;
They placed him near a window
So that he could enjoy the sun.
His carelessness became controlled;
They simply fed him from a wooden bowl.
Their young son viewed the scene with scorn.
And decided to carve a wooden bowl.
With a smile, his Mother asked him;
What are you making oh my son?
You look so intense; but it looks like fun.
Oh, yes, but I'll carve two;
Just like Grandpa's;
One for Dad and one for you.

By: Melvin Donaho

After writing the above poem, I decided to research the topic. While the poem was completely original; I did learn that there were two essays somewhat like what I had written and that Leo Tolstoy had written a similar theme but radically different and certainly not in poetry. Thus, I am content that although it would have been unknown to me, my poem is truly my own work and original.

Too Proud to Beg

Some sixty years ago in war torn Italy,
The fingers of poverty were ever present –
Even in once lovely Naples,
Now, shrouded in a pallor of grey.
American sailors, sightseeing ashore,
Risked being surrounded by her desperate poor;
Forced to stoop, to beg,
To sell their cherished treasures.
Attempting to be free, two hired a carriage;
An effort to view the city unencumbered.
God ruled otherwise – there was to be no escape.
While pausing for a stop sign,
There standing on the corner alone,
A stooped, elderly woman,
Destitute and forlorn;
A bunch of bruised bananas in her hand –
For sale – too proud to beg.
Overcome with sadness, I pondered:
What could she possibly need more,
Than to keep them for herself?
Motioning the driver to pause;
I bought her meager offering;
Accepting just two while motioning her
To keep the rest.

With tears streaming from her tired eyes,
She hugged and thanked me over and over.
Not a word I understood –
Her desperation lodged forever in my heart.
Kissing her weathered cheek,
I re-entered the carriage;
To be met with: why did you do that?
Here, have a banana.
You just don't understand …
She is a child of God in need –
Perhaps, someone's grandmother.
She could have been mine.
Twenty dollars must seem a mere token,
In the eyes of God.
For God cares; yes, God He cares,
Oh, surely God Almighty cares …

By: Mel Donaho

Tummy Rubs

I just found Truffles where I lay my head!
She's come to feel she owns the whole bed.
I'll not wrest her from her doggie nap
No, I shall dream of my love on my lap.
Truffles just turned and tossed and sighed;
Or, perhaps she's hearing the birdies outside.
Hmmm, I wonder if little doggies dream?
Perhaps of a tummy rub – all feet in the air
For a good tummy rub; a scratch on her ears;
She's been quite loyal for just under a year.
My Dear, can you guess what I'm thinking?
If you were only here:
I'd run my fingers through your hair.
And Truffles could whine and I wouldn't care.
But then there is you; wanting to be fair.
Rubbing her tummy; her feet in the air.

By: Melvin Donaho

Twice Blessed

Love passed away before my eyes;
Never to be held nor seen again
Yet, a lifetime of memories.
Remain behind.
Memories of how we came to meet;
Memories of our first kiss;
Oh so very sweet – true bliss
And then there came our wedding day;
With memories of a bride with her bouquet;
And the memories of that first night …
For sixty years as man and wife.
Ah yes, our Lord above;
Had blessed us with a life of love.
As wondrous as our life on Earth;
'Twas not so, our Savior's lowly birth;
He knew not love on evil earth
Yet He served and cured where er' he trod.
A wondrous Son for his Father, God.
And when they nailed Him to the cross;
'Though deep in pain;
He called out in his Father's name;
Forgive them; they know now what they do.
And thus, he died upon that cross;
Our sins forgiven; our souls not lost.
Yes, I'm twice blessed;
Her soul's in Heaven; as Christ's chosen guest.

By: Melvin Donaho

War's Betrayal

Today, I cried again;
Not for my beloved wife,
Now serving with our Lord;
But for my fellow man.
Called to serve in foreign-lands.
I see them sitting in the sun;
Recalling memories of not long ago
Thinking of what they would now find;
When they went home.
Indeed, war is hell!
To learn, the one you loved;
Your dearest love, you left behind;
Now learning upon return that she
Was unwilling to wait for thee.
Never mind the crashing sounds of war.
A heart can break and bleed much more.

By: Melvin Donaho

Your Picture on the Wall

My eyes are often led to view;
Your picture on the wall.
It now reflects your love, so true.
Your picture on the wall.
God sent us on our separate ways;
Your soul to be with Christ our Lord
While mine did here remain;
Your picture on the wall.
And when I look up at your face;
Fond memories I recall.
When God introduced me to a lass;
To become my love from Lincoln Hall.
How I remember that morning;
When I ran to beg your pardon;
For my housemate's rudeness
And crudeness to you the night before.
However, God did intervene;
He embraced us with loving arms;
He opened the Heavens and it poured.

As we ran to an inn next door.
Over coffee, I saw you change;
You asked me to attend church with you;
I asked; please, change your name.
With the loveliest of smiles upon your face;
To my surprise, you did reply;
"You'll have to ask my Dad, if it's ok."
With your parent's blessing;
We began our golden love.
After 60 years of wedded bliss;
God called to you from Heaven above.
Yet, He chose to leave me here;
Your picture on the wall;
With many nights in tears

By: Melvin Donaho

Printed in the United States
By Bookmasters